NO SUCH THING

AS OFF THE RECORD

www.mascotbooks.com

No Such Thing as OFF the Record

For more information, please contact:
Mascot Books
620 Herndon Parkway #320
Herndon, VA 20170
info@mascotbooks.com

Library of Congress Control Number: 2019909385

CPSIA Code: 978-1-64307-427-6
ISBN-13: PRV1219A

Printed in the United States

This book is dedicated to my mother, who is the epitome of an *extrovert*. She taught me to how to strike up a conversation and find relatability with almost anyone. The fearlessness I gleaned from her resulted in a lifelong love of public speaking and, ultimately, connecting with others.

To my daughters, who have so often witnessed and undoubtedly weathered untold embarrassment as I've befriended and chatted with complete strangers: thank you.

NO SUCH THING

AS OFF
THE RECORD

A **SURVIVAL GUIDE** FOR PUBLIC
SPEAKING AND MEDIA ENGAGEMENTS

ANDREA DEVAUX

CONTENTS

FOREWORD

Did you know that most people would rather die than speak in public? In a frequently quoted survey from *The Book of Lists*, it was revealed that out of a choice of several incredibly undesirable options presented to study participants, what people feared *the most* was not death, but rather it was the prospect of having to give a speech.

As you may have observed, our world is filled with a bombardment of lectures, speeches, cat videos, and breaking news. Within that smorgasbord of *attention getters*, it is painfully obvious that some media appearances are definitely more captivating than others. And most of you are probably thinking the cat videos are the winner.

All jokes aside, have you noticed how often speakers end up back-tracking on what they said, or end up having to "clarify" a misunderstood statement, only to have that misunderstanding become an even bigger issue or "message" than the one they had originally intended to present?

Folks not acquainted with the art of public speaking are often left feeling intimidated by the experience, usually preferring to shy away. In many instances there is a perception that some people are simply "gifted" at public speaking, and some are just, well...*not*. However, it is my assertion that looking good and sounding good in front of an audience are not some inborn talents. They are skills that can be learned.

Media interviews and speeches are, after all, an event, or more precisely, a type of theatre. In the case of a polished performance, we marvel at the effortless, authentic portrayal an actor brings to a role. Yet, *unless* we are proficient at the craft ourselves, the years of private coaching, along with research into the character, memorizing the lines and all that goes into being believable…all of those aspects of preparation are invisible. Even if you have been gifted with an abundance of talent, it won't make up for preparation, practice, and persistence.

A media appearance could easily be compared to an athletic event because many of the aspects required to excel when playing a sport are the same disciplines utilized to prepare for giving a talk or interview. In laying the groundwork for going in front of an audience, one must include the very same techniques that are employed to prepare for any sporting event:

1. Coaching
2. Practice
3. Wearing a uniform
4. Having a game plan
5. Studying your opponent

This book presents, in a straightforward manner, the techniques and tactics required to present a more interesting and engaging media appearance—one where you stay on track and say what you came to say. Nothing more, nothing less.

PART 1
The Media Interview

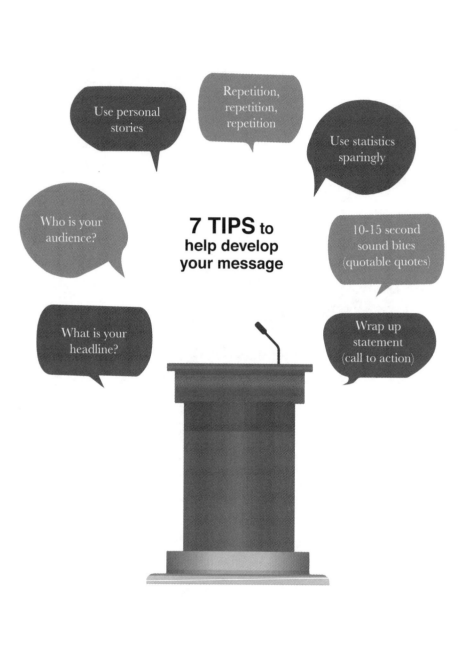

CHAPTER 1
Preparation

Understanding and navigating the sometimes-challenging terrain of a media interview will serve you well in any life situation, not just in your dealings with the public. *However,* having good interview skills is extremely important—especially if you are having to deal with inflammatory claims made against you or your organization.

Understanding how reporters tick, what types of questions you might be asked, *and* most importantly how to respond, will set you apart from your floundering peers.

The Message

Having a strong, clear message is absolutely crucial. Imagine you have an advertising campaign and you are spending hundreds of thousands of dollars (or possibly millions) on a 30-second commercial to be aired during the Super Bowl (or an equivalent, widely televised event in your country). You would make certain that you had a clear message about what you wanted your audience to know about you or your brand. Defining your message needs to be treated with the same reverence and attention to detail that you would use when preparing for an expensive television commercial.

The "message" is also known as the *SOCO*—the *Single Overriding Communications Objective.* The SOCO needs to have a beginning, middle, and end. How do you do that? Tell them what you are going to tell them, tell them, then tell them what you told them. This way, if your interview is edited, you have a fighting chance of getting your message across at least once. One main concept is all your audience will be able to digest, no matter how much information you try to cram in. Think: "less is more" when dealing with the media. Otherwise the more you try to add, the more diffused your message becomes.

And while we are on the topic of getting your message across, there are plenty of percentages tossed around regarding information retention—most of them quite misleading. So how much of what you say is actually retained by your audience? A seminal study from the University of Minnesota examined the listening ability of thousands of students and hundreds of business professionals. This research took decades and measured how much information listeners retained from a 10-minute presentation. Granted, not all presentations are the same and not all audience members are equally attentive, but just for giggles, here are the findings: Immediately after the presentation, listeners remembered 50 percent of what was said. And by the next day those same listeners only remembered 25 percent. Fast forward one week: 10 percent retention. If this and other similar studies are to be taken seriously, then making sure you have a strong message and finding many creative ways of sneaking *said message* into your talk or interview, the more successful you will be at having your message *stick* in the minds of your audience.

The following tips will help you formulate your message

- **Visualize your information as an article.** What is the headline? What would be the lead or attention-getting first sentence? Which points would you highlight? Your message should have an opening, a body, and a conclusion.

- **Be sure you can make your points in 30 seconds or less.**

- **Use repetition.** In real estate it's "location, location, location;" in media it's "repetition, repetition, repetition."

- **Think sound bites:** the easy-to-swallow and easy-to-remember statements. Sound bites should be memorable. *Don't bring the whole enchilada when all the media needs is the tortilla.* (See Chapter 9 for sound bite development.)

- **Draft 8 to 10 interview questions** or suggestions to help guide the interviewer towards the material you came to talk about. Offer your suggestions humbly.

- **Develop support statements** for any assertions you will make.

- **Practice stating your major objective.** Be ready to say it two or three times during an interview, but make it sound different to the audience each time.

- **Use personal experience** to back up your statements. Who can refute that? Also use second person "you" or third person "they" to make your message sound more personal.

- **By all means use statistics and numbers,** but make them relevant. And better to speak in generalities or averages rather than getting bogged down with too many specifics. For example: *"Almost one third of all Americans are considered obese,"* instead of *"160 million Americans or 31.6% of adult males and females aged 34 to 64 are considered obese."*

- **Be strategic with the timing of your message.** Gear it to public's interest, not your peers' interests. Consider whether the date of your talk or interview relates to broader public interest in your message. In some instances, you may be able to tie a season or holiday and weave that into the fabric of your talk, therefore capturing wider media attention. If you were giving an interview about some kind of cause or public service announcement, then it behooves you to maximize the impact of your message by taking advantage of notable dates.

» An example of this was when the U.S. Women's Soccer Team chose to sue U.S. Soccer for gender discrimination, citing inequalities over pay and working conditions. On any day this would already be *news*. But the women's team didn't do this on just any day. They did it on March 8th, capitalizing on International Women's Day and therefore, maximizing the scope of media attention by choosing a day when news outlets were already looking for topics specifically relating to women's issues.

By incorporating noteworthy dates and tying them in with your message, this can not only add prominence to what you are speaking about, but also potentially reach a much wider audience.

- **Prepare a wrap-up statement for your message.** Something that encapsulates your main points. This may be as simple as repeating the name of your business while you are thanking the interviewer for their time. For example, "On behalf of myself and the staff at Widgets International, we are honored to have this opportunity."

CHAPTER 2
What Makes News?

The media is often criticized for being overly negative (or at least it can seem that way) and here's why: "The *news* is the *not!*" News stories about what is *not* going well catch our attention and—let's face it—in our own lives we are just the same. When there is something happening that is different from the usual, we tend to put our focus on it.

To illustrate my point, I remember one Halloween a few years back I took my two young daughters trick or treating. We must have walked in and out of several dozen houses all in effort to increase their candy stash…and of course show off our costumes. Yes, being a theatre geek, I too was sporting a themed Halloween outfit. Most of the houses were decked out in various degrees of "scary" ghoulish decorations…however, the one house I remember to this day is the one that had a huge spider on the roof. It was as if a massive arachnid was attempting to capture and devour the entire house. My witch's hat went off to those homeowners, who clearly went out of their way to freak out a bunch of costumed toddlers! Yet, it also epitomizes what makes news: News is about something that is different and *not* the usual. So, if 100 planes land safely into Heathrow International Airport, it's no big deal. However, if one of those planes crashes whilst landing, then it's all over the news, and that's what everyone will be talking about.

Another example close to home for me was prompted by an announcement regarding air quality. In California over the past few years we have experienced several catastrophic wildfires. Each year is worse than the previous. Whilst writing this chapter, the most devastating fire in California's history was still not even at 50 percent containment, and on the news we were informed that the San Francisco Bay Area's air quality was the worst in the world. Yet, when the air is clean and fresh, it's a non-issue.

Conversely, in New Delhi, the opposite is true. The air quality is usually so bad that it is only newsworthy when air quality improves. My point being, what makes news is all about what's new or different. Therefore, if you are being contacted by the media because of something perceived to be a negative, make sure you are prepared to share what you are doing to make things right, fix the situation, or to make improvements for next time. Even in catastrophic situations, so many amazing and heartwarming human-interest stories can come out of tragedy. In other words, bring your own "new or different" response so that the focus turns from a negative situation into what hopefully will, in time, be a positive outcome.

What makes a newsworthy event?

1. Uniqueness
2. Timeliness
3. Public Interest (including heartwarming/ human interest stories)
4. Twist/odd juxtaposition of things ("man bites dog")
5. Sex
6. Achievement/Recognition
7. Breaking news story
8. Conflict
9. Superlatives
10. Celebrities

Use the following criteria for making news:

Organize your message according to a news reporter's key questions:

Who?

Who is this about?

What?

What is this about?

When?

When did it happen?

Where?

Where did it happen?

Why?

Why is this newsworthy?

How?

How did it happen?

CHAPTER 3
Goals

What are the reporters' goals?

- To get the story they think will interest their audience
- To meet their deadline
- To help their audience understand what you are saying
- To get you to say what they want you to say
- To probe for:
  - » Information *(Tell me the details…)*
  - » Clarification *(What exactly do you mean?)*
  - » Justification *(What is the reasoning behind that?)*
  - » Argumentation *(Polls reflect a downturn in your popularity!)*

What are your goals?

- To *educate* the public
- To *communicate* one or two major points
- To *promote* a positive image of yourself, your profession, your company or organization

CHAPTER 4
Formula for Success

How to create a win-win with news reporters

- Availability and punctuality
- Knowledge
- Honesty
- Brevity
- Enthusiasm

Meeting deadlines

Reporters need news *now*. It won't do any good to call the next day and say, "I'm ready," especially if it is a topic that you are reluctant to speak about. Being prompt gives you a chance to have a say in how the story goes.

- Ask the reporter their deadline, then meet it.
- Be available on short notice.
- Get to the station early.

CHAPTER 5
The Audience

"The best audience is intelligent,
well-educated, and a little drunk."
–Alben W. Barkley

Who is your audience?

Give some thought to who your audience might be, what mood they will be in, and the conditions under which they will be listening to you. This will help you tailor your message so that it has the best chance of being understood and well-received.

- Ask who makes up the audience.

- Is it for print, broadcast, social media, et cetera?

- What is the venue like?

  » Studio/ site of your choosing/ on location?

  » Where is the location?

  » Will it be live or prerecorded?

  » Phone/ Skype/ Zoom?

If it is a live taping for TV or radio, then be aware that with any faux pas, the repercussions can be immediate. If it's for print, (be it newspaper or internet) or a periodical publication, which is slightly less urgent, you will have some wiggle room regarding how you present your information and what gets edited out.

Remember to talk through the reporter to your audience. Here's an example from my own life: When I was working for a major medical organization as a media coach, I was consulting high-powered doctors to prepare to go on camera. Many of these doctors were extremely gifted specialists, however they were not so great when it came to communicating with us *mere mortals*. These doctors would often try to impress their audience, as if they were speaking to other doctors. I often had to encourage and remind them that other doctors were *not* their target audience—therefore they needed to drop the jargon (i.e. don't use industry language or medical terms) and speak to their audience as if they were speaking to a patient. So, when I say *"speak through the reporter,"* I mean speak to the reporter as if they were your audience.

CHAPTER 6
Strategy

Just as you would prepare for any sporting event, a media appearance requires preparation for "the big game."

These preparations include:

- Developing a game plan

- Practicing

- Coaching

- Focusing on strengths

- Identifying and addressing weaknesses

- Choosing a uniform

- Studying your opponent

- Mentally preparing

Let's discuss each of these in a little more depth:

Develop a game plan

- Ask for the complete name of the publication or program.

- Ask what the topic is and the reporter's angle on the story.

- Ask who else will be interviewed for the article or program.

- Become familiar with the program or publication you will be appearing in, and the listeners or readers it reaches.

Practice

- Practice with a colleague, a friend, your spouse, or partner.
- Practice using video or audio recording features on your phone…practice, practice, practice. If possible, practice in the location where you will do the interview. Record yourself, listen for problem areas—recognition is the first step to solving problems.
- Study all sides of the topic or issue. Identify potential "hot buttons" and prepare your responses to them.
- Warm-up by humming, singing, or talking before the interview begins.
- You may need to project your voice just a bit more than you normally would during the interview.
- How you feel affects how you sound, so make sure you feel great before the interview. Get proper rest, eat well (such as a meal high in protein and vegetables and low in carbohydrates, since carbs can make some people feel tired,) take a brisk walk to get your blood flowing, and think positively.
- Practice a conversational style that will work under fire or confrontation. Have a friend or family member shoot questions at you—the kinds of questions you would *hate* to get. Get comfortable with being uncomfortable by being ready for the worst. Chances are, it won't end up being that bad, but it's always wise to be ready for challenging questions.
- Do interviews with local radio and public access stations. Give speeches at business groups such as Rotary, Business Network International, Toast Masters, et cetera—any group that presents speakers. I have listed several suggested groups in the "Resources" section at the end of this book.

Coaching

As with any field, getting coaching is imperative *if* you plan on taking everything you are doing to the next level. There are many advantages in having a public speaking coach.

First, it gives you a deadline to have your message or speech ready by. Procrastinators out there take heed! Knowing you will have to practice your prepared talk or interview with a coach will hopefully light the fire under your heinie to get your thoughts in order and start practicing.

Secondly, it gives you an opportunity to put your speech or interview on its feet, and get immediate feedback as well as receive important insights on things that you might be saying and repetitive mannerisms or body language that you were unaware of. Even just a couple of hours with a good coach will make a *huge* difference. Trust me, this is not the area to skimp out on.

Focus on strengths

Regardless of the subject of your talk or interview, it is essential that you put your focus on what strengths you possess. Whenever possible, use imagery to help reinforce those points. Do not get sidetracked into talking about your competition or speaking about things you don't know much about. When in doubt, state what is important and why. State what you, your project, program or company have to offer that is unique or different.

Identify and address weaknesses

Problems can also be known as your weak areas. Perhaps they are something you are not very proud of; perhaps something embarrassing; or, something that went wrong. There are two ways to handle problems: trivializing and globalizing.

Example of trivializing:
"It doesn't happen very often and it's the exception, not the rule."
Example of globalizing:
"It's not just my problem but it's everyone's—it's society's problem."

Pay attention the next time you hear the news about an oil spill, a politician caught in some kind of scandal, or a company found at fault for something. Notice how they handle these uncomfortable media situations. Do they embrace the situation? Do they say "no comment?" *Or* do they use one of the above-mentioned techniques?

Choose a uniform

Knowing the setting and the audience is key when deciding what to wear. As with most sports, a uniform lets everyone know what sport you are playing and which team you are on. With media, wearing the appropriate clothing is just as important. In Chapter 8, greater detail of this topic is covered. If you get a say in the matter, always choose colors that flatter you. Not sure what looks good on you? Ask yourself what you have worn in the past that people have complimented you on. Still need help? An image consultant or personal stylist might be a wise investment—at the very least to find a couple of appropriate outfits for upcoming media appearances and interviews.

Study your opponent

Possibly the least known of the skills required to be ready for a media appearance. You need to know all sides of the story, which includes knowing what your competition is saying and/or doing. This does not mean you will be putting your focus or time talking about your opponent, however knowing their strategy or game plan is crucial in helping you hone in on what you offer that is better or different. In an interview scenario it means you are less likely to be caught like a deer in the headlights when responding to a question about what the other side is up to.

Mental preparation

This is where the rubber meets the road when it comes to appearing comfortable in front of an audience. Talk yourself out of your nervousness. Most speakers give themselves mental pep talks while they're waiting to go on camera or on stage.

Here are some suggestions:

- Remind yourself of positive things people have said to you. You may want to keep encouraging letters and cards from friends and loved ones that you have received over the years. Read them when your self-esteem needs a boost!

- Tell yourself something that makes you feel better about yourself such as: *"I know more about this topic than anyone here!"* If you find yourself getting off track from your prepared statements, calm your nerves by reminding yourself that nobody else knows what you planned to say. Also putting the focus on your audience and truly being of service helps many speakers overcome nerves. A humbling reminder: you are simply here to share your knowledge.

- Tell yourself you look amazing, you are intelligent, and you've put a lot of work into creating this moment. Whatever you say to yourself, make sure those statements are positive. And repeat them to yourself silently as you would with a "mantra."

Stuart Smalley, a character from long ago on *Saturday Night Live,* had a mantra that you might want to adopt: *"I'm good enough, I'm smart enough, and gosh darn it, people like me!"*

CHAPTER 7
Reporter "Tricks"

Now granted, not all reporters employ these "tricks," but certainly their goal is to get a good interview and if you're not giving it, you may find they will use some of the following techniques to get something interesting out of you.

- Playing dumb

- Asking inflammatory questions/making inflammatory statements

- Putting words in your mouth

- Silence

- Asking the same questions over and over

To break this down more specifically, the following are 12 tough questions that you might find yourself hearing in a more investigative reporting session.

12 Interview Challenges

(and how to deal)

I. Know-it-all questions

You will have two kinds of questions: open-ended or closed-ended. A question that requires a *"yes"* or *"no"* answer is a closed-ended. Often the reporter plans to present a certain viewpoint and wants you simply to confirm it with a *"yes"* or *"no."* Avoid this situation by supplying the reporter with your own message, not confirming nor denying theirs.

Let's suppose you are in the financial sector and you were fielding this question:

"Are you happy with the latest jobs report?"

Instead of responding with a "yes" or "no," you might say:

"At (name of organization or company) we welcome a good jobs report however numbers like these can often be skewed due to the fact that many folks have given up looking for work—and so it may not be an entirely accurate representation of what is really going on in the economy."

Give your answer in a complete sentence which includes the name of the company (reinforcing brand) and something that links the response to a message that you wish to convey.

II. Multiple-part questions

"What about this, what about that, and what about the other thing?"

With multi-part questions, answer only one. Hopefully the question that most closely ties in with your message. If the reporter really wants to know the other questions, they will ask again.

III. Repetition

Asking the same question over and over again.

You say, *"As I've said before, this is the same question...What I said was..."*

That should get them off your back! One would only use this under extremely hostile conditions.

IV. Speculation

Beware of queries beginning with *"What if....?"* or speaking hypothetically.

The "Let's pretend…" scenario.
You say, *"That's not the point here…"*

Another option: *"I prefer not to answer hypothetical questions…but what I can say is…"* (and go on with your message)

V. Leading

This is when the reporter telegraphs the expected answer.

"Aren't you angry that your business is losing money because people are eating healthier?"

They will try to put words in your mouth. Never say, *"No comment."*
You say, *"I'd like to answer that question but…"* and give the reporter something they can live with. Examples of this would be when there might be pending litigation or circumstances that prevent you from divulging the details.

Another tactic would be to say:

"What I'm really trying to say is…"
or
"I think it would be more accurate to say…"

VI. Loaded questions

The first part of the question is not to your liking or is incorrect. These *"When did you stop beating your spouse?"* type of questions are likely intended to draw you out.

"People I've talked to say that minorities can't get a fair shake in your company."
Or, *"Your organization only allows women to be members. Does that mean you discriminate against men?"*

A possible response to the above question might be:

"Our organization provides a safe space for women to network and do business together. Many of our members have had traumatic experiences in male dominated environments or in some instances have religious reasons for not choosing to socialize with men in a business setting."

Notice the response specifically did not go down the rabbit hole where the reporter was headed, instead choosing to respond with empathy and compassion, intentionally taking the interview in a different direction.

With loaded questions, simply correct the misinformation and give the facts, unemotionally. You can fulfill the media's quest for drama in another way—by being animated and interesting, using statements with imagery or anecdotes, having props, et cetera.

VII. Either/Or

When a question is presented as a choice between two negative options such as having to choose between making deep cuts in social programs versus incurring untenable national debt, do not fall for having to respond with choosing one or the other. It's rarely that simple. If you really are at a loss on how to respond, use this opportunity to speak about what is really important (aka your message).

Literally, you say:
"What's important here is…"
or
"Here's the real problem…"

or

"It boils down to this…"

or

"What matters the most in this type of situation…"

An example:

"Does this administration want people tortured or bombed?"

Either answer is not going to be good. Steer back to your main message: *"What's important to our administration is that nobody gets hurt…"* and move on with what you came to talk about.

VIII. Silence

Silence makes people uncomfortable. It is an invitation to keep talking. You might say things you didn't plan on saying. Never say more than you have to. Instead, use the silence to reinforce earlier points, or use examples to back up your main message.

IX. Labeling

"Don't you think your organization's ideas about world peace are just a tad unrealistic in today's trigger-happy world?"

All labels are simplistic. Avoid repeating or accepting them. Come prepared with your own, in the form of sound bites.

In this scenario you could say something like,

"Our organization believes that life is precious. At the heart, we all desire peace, not only for ourselves but for future generations."

X. Naivety or feigned ignorance

The reporter doesn't know much:

"Gosh, I know nothing about your cause. Tell me everything..."

Here's a chance to present your own agenda, but keep it simple. Remember: Tell them what you are going to tell them, tell them, and then tell them what you told them. Also, it's always a good idea to have media kits available, bios, and information about your organization's history.

XI. Friendly

There is no such thing as *off the record!*

If you don't want it repeated, don't say it.

- Not at lunch with a reporter.

- Not if the reporter is your best friend.

- Not if you've been promised it will remain off the record.

- Not if you've asked to be kept anonymous.

Possibly one of the most infamous examples of this was a taped interview in 1995 between Mrs. Kathleen Gingrich, 68, and American journalist and reporter Connie Chung. Chung asked Mrs. Gingrich what her son, Newt, had to say about then President Clinton.

That question then led to the following exchange:

Mom Gingrich: "Nothing, and I can't tell you what he said about Hillary."

Chung: "You can't?"

Mom Gingrich: "I can't."

Chung: "Why don't you just whisper it to me, just between you and me?"

Mom Gingrich: (In a loud whisper) "She's a bitch. About the only thing he ever said about her."

Ms. Chung was not entirely honest when she said "just between you and me." The cameras were still rolling. What Chung really meant to say was something like: *"Just between you and me and the millions of people who will be tuning in to my show!"*

Many executives in the television industry went on to say that it was probably 68-year-old Gingrich's own fault, and that she should have realized that with the cameras still recording, anything she said was *on the record*. Albeit she was from a different generation and had trusted that what she was saying would not go further. She could not have been more sorely mistaken.

XII. False assumptions

"Since your earnings are down 50 percent, can you confirm…"

The unwary respondent might say, *"My earnings are only down 20 percent…"*

Such a response would thus give away information the respondent had not planned on sharing with the media.

XIII. The irrelevant study

"Several reports say companies like yours will be left in the dust a year from now. What say you?"

These types of questions might be a trap. It could be an irrelevant study or something made up. Don't pretend to know what they are referring to. If you're not familiar with the study and the reporter is, you're going to get nailed.

You say, *"I'm not familiar with that study, but what I do know is…"*

XIV. Finishing up

"Goodbye."

Even if the interview has ended, you are still on the record. Be very careful. Thank them for their time and let the reporter know how to reach you for any follow-up questions or clarifications. Don't allow yourself to fall into a more chatty or informal conversation. You don't know if the sound is still recording or the cameras are still on…including cell phone cameras.

CHAPTER 8
Appearance

According to Albert Mehrabian, Professor Emeritus of Psychology at UCLA, famous for his work on the relative importance of verbal and non-verbal messages, audiences receive and respond to information from these three sources in the following ratios:

- words account for 7 percent

- tone of voice accounts for 38 percent

- body language accounts for 55 percent

Knowing what you want to say is one thing. How you get that information across in a way that is *impression-making* is another. Finding that balance between being visually interesting at the same time as setting a professional tone is extremely important.

Many years ago, I was coaching someone who worked for a nonprofit in San Francisco. Her organization was a grassroots group that was helping troubled youth get off the streets and into training programs to improve their skills. The nonprofit was doing amazing work in the community and she would often have to go on television to represent her organization.

To be clear, this woman's personal style was very different from what I suggested she adopt for her media appearances. For example, she would arrive at coaching sessions wearing flowy cotton dresses with bells sewn into the fabric, Birkenstock sandals, no makeup, and long, rather messy hair—a "hippie" look. To her credit she was an amazing person as well as an amazing speaker; very passionate about what her organization was accomplishing.

I advised her to wear something professional, to pull her hair back, use a bit of powder for the shine and some color for lips and cheeks. She was incensed and stated that adopting that "look" would not be personally authentic. I reminded her that representing oneself or one's organization in the media is not the time to be choosing an outfit that expresses your artistic side (unless being an artist is what you do). Representing your organization on camera requires wearing a *uniform* which invites your audience to take both you and your organization seriously.

With this in mind, I suggested she do a practice interview wearing what she thought would show her personality best and then later in the day do an interview where she adopted more professional attire and together we would play back and see what looked best.

The result was interesting. We both noticed an extreme difference between her media appearance from the morning, when she was wearing her usual garb, compared to later when she adopted a more professional-looking outfit. When wearing her free-spirited attire, she would get very serious whilst she was speaking. All the fun and joy about what her organization was up to would disappear when the camera was rolling. We discovered that because she didn't look professional, unconsciously she spent her energy trying to be taken seriously.

When she complied with the coaching for the afternoon interview—put her hair back, wore a jacket, and used a small amount of makeup (to add color that the camera tends to wash out,) the difference was astounding. She no longer had to subliminally convince her audience that she was serious. This allowed her to be more relaxed in the role of representing her group and speaking to the amazing things they were doing in the world. Ultimately this allowed her the freedom to let her personality shine in ways that her usual clothing choices did not.

It is important to stress that the following pointers are based on giving an interview in a professional setting. If you are known for having an eclectic style (and that style may be your trademark,) then consider that some of these suggestions may not be relevant for you. I do believe, even when finding a professional look, that the outfit you choose expresses and encompasses both your professionalism and your personality. That may take the form of a colorful scarf or fun tie—something that you love. However, if what you love to wear are sweatpants and a baggy tee shirt...then better to stick with my suggestions. Agreed?

Recommendations for all speakers

- Make sure your appearance is appropriate.

- For television interviews, everybody should have compact powder available to keep the shine off your face (or bald spot). If you are not familiar with how to find a color that will match, any department store cosmetics counter will be happy to assist you. The main thing to remember is to choose a shade that is close to your natural coloring.

- Accept makeup in the studio if it is offered. Feel free to inquire as to whether there will be hair and makeup stylists available to you at the location.

- Jackets give the wearer added authority. Also, the collar of a jacket is a good place to secure the lavalier microphone.

- Stay away from fabrics and patterns that "dance" (moray) on camera such as herringbones, checks, polka dots, tweeds, and dark and light combinations of stripes or prints.

- Avoid black clothing and also white clothing. Both of those choices are too color contrasting.

- Avoid flashy jewelry and expensive pens.

- Keep clothing free of pins, name-tags, etc.

- Make sure that there are as few folds around your middle as possible. Simply stated, tug down on the front of your shirt or jacket, right before you begin.

- Empty all bulky items from pockets.

- Eyeglasses: If you have contacts, wear them. If not, avoid sunglasses, light-sensitive glasses, glasses with heavy frames, or bifocals. Tortoise shell glasses or rimless glasses work well. If you are doing a lot of media appearances you may want to consider an anti-glare coating on your glasses.

- If you have hair that hangs in your eyes, glasses that constantly slip down, dingy teeth, or unmanicured fingernails, all of these send an unkempt message that you don't care about yourself— or your audience.

Masculine Style Recommendations

- Wear a suit or jacket; dark blue is preferable.

- Shirts should be neatly pressed, a solid color—light blue is best, with a button-down or stiff collar (to avoid the collar flipping up). Avoid knit polo shirts that rumple and look disheveled. Button the jacket if you can. If the jacket cannot be buttoned, straighten it after sitting.

- If you have a bald spot, have compact powder standing by to keep the shine off.

- Trim facial hair and get a haircut. Mustaches often make a person look slightly grumpy so be mindful to smile. If you tend to get "Five o'clock shadow," keep an electric razor handy.

- Socks should be knee high so skin will not show when legs are crossed. The color of your socks should be a darker shade than your pants.

- Wear a bold tie. This helps to "pop" attention up to the face. Make sure your collar and tie are straight and shirt is tucked in. Wear a bowtie only if this is your style. Avoid close collars and ties that choke.

- Don't show a bare chest. Even if you are a doctor and in an interview wearing scrubs, try to avoid the "chest hair peaking up out of your shirt" scenario. If you are particularly hairy, consider a tee shirt underneath.

Feminine Style Recommendations

- Makeup: Add a little more color to lips and cheeks than usual. Even if your normal style is not to wear any makeup, understand that when you go on camera, it tends to make people look a bit washed out. More definition and color will help make you look more engaged, energetic and alive.

- Keep in mind that the television crew will need a lapel or equally accessible place to clip a microphone. Silky dresses or blouses are difficult to work with. V-necks work well on camera, but no cleavage or plunging necklines! If wearing a skirt or dress, wear one long enough so you don't have to think about it. Darker pantyhose are preferable.

- Solid white blouses or white dresses without jackets are unflattering. The camera person will need to balance exposure against your face and if you are wearing bright white clothing, it will cause the image to glow in a way that could be distracting. Remember, you want the focus to be on your face, not your clothing.

- Jewelry is fine, but no long, dangling earrings. Do not wear necklaces that can clunk against a lavalier microphone. Watch out for ostentatious jewelry or "statement" pieces—unless it is in line with your brand or personality, it might come across as distracting.

- Television likes colors. Good strong colors are green, blue, purple, coral, and small amounts of red. If possible, find out the color of the set and choose colors that will stand out, yet be complementary to your surroundings.

CHAPTER 9
Body Language

Eye contact is critical to effective communication. Look the interviewer in the eye and maintain eye contact when listening. When part of a panel discussion, look straight ahead or at the person speaking. If seated between two others, be it reporters on either side of you, or other panelists, avoid "tennis-match" head turning; choose one person to focus on for a while and then naturally turn to the other one. If they are bantering back and forth while you are "piggy in the middle," then look straight ahead or down.

Only look directly at the camera when you are doing a remote interview where you are in a studio or on location and the reporter is in a different locale. Sometimes these types of interviews are edited in such a way that both of you appear on screen at the same time. Some news shows put three or four people on screen, side by side, at the same time. Surprisingly some of those folks do not act like they realize the camera is on them the whole time. If you are in one of these scenarios and need to look directly at the camera, make sure to put in your mind's eye, a person that you think would want to hear what you have to say "into the lens" so it doesn't just feel like you are looking into a black hole. Creating, with your imagination, a friendly audience member, will help give your responses more warmth and translate as you being more personable.

If you are listening to a question or response from another participant, make sure to still remain engaged—nodding and otherwise being a support to what is being said. If you don't agree with what is being said, try not to contort your face in disapproval but rather stay neutral and unaffected. Our political leaders have given us many colorful examples of what *not to do* in this sort of situation. No eye rolling!

Body language tips to remember:

- Use your hands naturally, or more precisely to demonstrate certain points. Remember to bring your hands up within the frame of the shot. This will make you appear more involved and enthusiastic about the interview. Don't point; use open hand gestures instead.

- Feel free to ask what the framing is so you will know exactly what kind of range of motion you have. If the camera is framed in a medium shot then you have free rein to move your hands anywhere waist height and above; medium close up—that means your hands will need to come up higher than mid chest and closer to your face. If you are in a close up, then your hands will need to be around your face. This is important since without knowing what the framing is, you may be adding wonderful gestures to emphasize your points but they don't end up in the shot. All of your efforts would be for naught!

- Maintain your focus. Don't be distracted by lights, photographers, audio people, and equipment. Concentrate on the interviewer or reporter, and maintain eye contact.

- Be aware of your body language (especially facial expressions) as well as your tone—keep your voice natural and animated.

- Remain calm, professional, and positive. Even if the interviewer becomes skeptical, argumentative, or deliberately tries to stimulate controversy. Maintain composure.

- Take a few deep breaths to relax and use very slight pauses throughout. You need to sound in control—like you are having a conversation with a colleague about a subject you are passionate about.

The seated interview

- Sit up straight with your butt back in the chair and lean slightly forward to look more attentive.

- Leg options: Cross legs (or feet at the ankles) after sitting and place hands on the knees. Bear in mind that some folks unconsciously "wag" one leg when it is crossed so if that is you, and you absolutely *have* to cross your legs, then glue the top leg to the bottom one. This was a technique I learned at finishing school. (My parents sent me when I was 18, since from their perspective I was on the verge of becoming a hippie! I never realized until later in life, how useful some of those ideas would end up being!) Search images of the British royal family "leg crossing" for examples of this method.

- Alternatively, you can sit with legs together. All genders should watch for not having a wide distance between the legs. (This conveys an unconscious message of taking up space.) And consider, if sitting beside others, gaping legs with the groin area exposed could be deemed disrespectful. If wearing a skirt or a dress, obviously the reason for having legs close together need not be explained…*unless* you are Sharon Stone's character in *Basic Instinct*'s famous leg-uncrossing scene!

- Keep away from the "fig leaf" (hands clasped at crotch), or the "school boy" (hands clasped behind back, as if to say, "I'm in trouble"). You always want your hands "unlocked" and ready to use.

The standing interview

- Use the "runner position:" one foot slightly forward of the other—almost an "L" shape with the feet.

- Check that you are standing straight. Even tilting your head to the side slightly or bending too far forward can put a strain on your throat. Roll your shoulders back and let them drop down.

- Let your hands rest at your sides or leave one loosely holding your lapel to remind you that your hand is there and you need to be using it. It's okay to have one hand in a pocket, but make sure all coins/items are emptied from pockets to avoid "jingling." (It's okay to have one coin if you must play with something to help alleviate nervousness!)

- Again, as with the seated interview, the same advice about hands applies for the standing interview. Avoid "fig leaf" hands, or the "school boy" hands. Keep hands "unlocked" and ready to use.

Avoid the following

- Inappropriate smiling or laughter
- Tightly clasped hands or gripping sides of chairs, tables, knees
- Toying with pencils, water glasses, buttons, microphones
- Leaning forward into the microphone (panel discussion)
- Drumming fingers on tabletop
- Tightening and loosening jaw
- Looking around the studio or at TV monitors
- Sitting ramrod straight with an unnatural posture
- Slouching

- Swinging legs
- Shifting or swiveling in chair

Exercises to help you relax

Being a part-time fitness instructor, I often utilize yoga exercises with my clients. The following are proven stress reducers.

1. During neck stretches, tilt your head back and as you do open your mouth and relax your throat. Imagine you are a cat about to get your chin scratched. This is a great stretch for helping the throat muscles loosen. Neutralize that stretch by then bringing your chin to your chest for a few breaths, then gently bring your head back to neutral.

2. Do directional head stretches. While keeping your shoulders back and down, move your head slowly forward then back to center; to the sides and back to center; tilt back, then back to center; finally chin down then back to center.

3. Bend forward from the waist as if you were a rag doll, shake your arms, and then sway them loosely side to side as if your arms were the branches of a weeping willow tree. Let your head drop and relax your neck. Then stand up straight rolling up, one vertebra at a time. Breathe in deeply, hold for a beat, then exhale.

4. Never underestimate the power of a good, brisk walk to get rid of excess nerves and energy.

5. Relax your breath. Breathe in slowly, hold for a beat, breath out slowly, and hold for a beat. Repeat 5-10 times. Even just a few of these intentional breaths will have a calming effect. Yawning, even a fake yawn, can be a helpful calming yet energizing exercise. Energizing because of the increased oxygen intake.

CHAPTER 10
How to Say
What You Want to Say

One cannot emphasize enough how much "information competition" there is in the media. Help the interviewer out with slow, careful explanations, and use the phrase, *"Let me tell you why this is so important."* At the core, this is what all reporters are trying to determine: Why is this important?

- Offer generous responses: Give more than just an answer. Give an answer plus your message.

  Question = Answer + 1

- Be friendly. Answer in the positive as much as possible.

- Listen before speaking.

- Respond to the interviewer "in the moment." Be present.

- State your most important fact at the beginning.

- Be patient and polite, never arrogant.

- Speak with enthusiasm, conviction, emotion.

- Speak only for yourself. Alternatively, if you are speaking for your company or organization, make certain you are aware of its position, especially with regard to controversial issues.

- "Project" yourself into a more familiar, comfortable setting. Imagine you are talking with a friend, an associate, a kind neighbor…someone with whom you feel comfortable talking.

- Help the listener by using repetition, outlines, summaries, examples, and appropriate levity. Use imagery. For example, you might say a hole was "about the size of a quarter" rather than "small."

- Begin your answer by rephrasing the question.

- Be brief and to the point.

- Be original. Have a fresh, strong opinion.

- If your interview is being pre-recorded, feel free to ask the reporter if you can go again (or even have several takes.) The worst they can say is no.

- Keep your notes handy. Index cards can be helpful but don't read. Use as a reference only.

- Use examples. Interesting stories about real people bring your information to life, and nobody can refute it. Sharing real life stories is an excellent way to reiterate your message in a way that is compelling and original.

- Don't get sidetracked. Pick two or three key points you want to make and try to make them early in the interview. Repeat them at least once through the course of the interview and, if possible, at the end of the interview.

- Always sound like you are delighted to be interviewed.

- Convey your respect for your interviewer and listeners. Have a conversation, don't lecture or pontificate.

- Stay away from insider jargon.

- Listen carefully and be prepared to respond to lead-ins. Use every question as an opportunity to launch into one of your planned mini-speeches. Bridge questions to fit your message into a response. Bridging is a phrase, clause, or sentence that moves you away from the question to a preferred position. For example: "Let's consider the larger issue here," or "I don't know much about that, but what I do know is…"

- Consider your response before you start to speak. Focus on the main point you want to communicate. Use pauses before your response and during to allow the audience to catch up with your ideas and to punctuate certain points.

- Do not answer with "yes," "no," "absolutely," or any other word that is not part of a complete sentence. By answering in a complete sentence, your responses can be used as stand-alone statements or sound bites. And make sure that you pause before beginning your response so that the reporter's question can be edited out. If you respond too quickly, there could be overlap which might cause editing issues, and your statement may not end up being used, regardless of how good it is.

- Use *"and"* or *"however"* to address adverse or hostile questions. These are transition words, along with others such as *"again," "moreover," "in light of…"* and many more. Transition words are very useful when used to get you from one place to another…*for example*, the reporter's hostile question over to your message. It quickly hop-scotches you over to a different point of view without *going there* and being pigeonholed into having to answer their specific question.

- Make certain the question is appropriate. Before you answer, correct any misinformation, misstatements, or incorrect assumptions.

- Don't hesitate to ask for clarification of a question.

- Disarm a hostile interviewer with smiles and kindness and by using bridging techniques to convey your message.

- Use humor if it's valid, but be careful! Any joke can potentially offend someone, so it's better to use situational jokes. An example of a situational joke I use when I teach a weight lifting class at a local gym is when we are doing an exercise called *upright row*. I remind folks to keep their weights close to their body and come up with the hands to mid chest, or mid nipple…whichever comes first. As you can probably tell, some of my jokes are a bit of a groaner…but they help everyone get through a necessary evil: working out for an hour. And laughter is always great way to help ease the pain.

- Have available a glass of water or hot tea with lemon. Beverages or foods containing dairy can make your voice sound gluggy. Avoid consuming alcohol before the interview. Eat lightly—a heavy meal can make breathing more labored and bring your energy down.

- Emphasize important words, underlining them with your voice, so that your meaning will be clear to your audience. A shift in emphasis can reinforce or change a meaning. To illustrate my point, say this sentence: *"She said she did not take his money."* Change where you put the emphasis on each different word… et voila! You get a completely different meaning each time.

- Be a performer. You need a bit of drama to entice people to listen. Project your personality.

- Bring props. This will add motivation for using your hands. Remember to ask what size the camera (or cameras) are framed at so your props will be seen within the shot. If using props, make sure the producer and director know about them. Know how you plan to use them on camera.

- When the red light is on, the camera is on. Come alive.

Voice

- Does your voice sound strong? Record your talk or prepared statements and listen to yourself. If you sound calm and assured, warm and easygoing, then you are good to go. If you don't like what you hear, check that your posture is good. Make sure you're not only getting your breath, but allowing your breathing to punctuate your words.

- Some people end up speaking too fast when they get nervous while others become dumbstruck when placed in front of an audience. Work on your pacing to prevent either extreme. This will enable you to use your voice to emphasize or *underline* the points you want to stand out. When most people give a talk or go on camera, they tend to speed up their natural speaking style. By choosing to speak slowly, by using pacing and pauses for emphasis, what you came to say will be digested more easily by the audience and more of what you say will be remembered. When in doubt, slow down.

- High-pitched tones can sound nervous or childish. Lower sounding voices convey confidence. If you have a higher pitched voice you will want to practice deliberately lowering your voice. Using breathing exercises and meditation techniques can help. Please see Chapter 27 for a deeper dive into the topics of voice and pacing.

CHAPTER 11
Sound Bites

Take an ordinary sentence and make it memorable

News sound bites are "stand alone." The reporter's questions or interviewer's voice will not be heard. Therefore, compose your answer as a complete sentence that can stand by itself. Preparing sound bites also can be very similar to preparing an "elevator pitch."

Let's recap

Who is my audience?

What is my message?

How can I put those messages into sound bites?

- Think *10-* to *15-second* chunks of information.

- Use an *analogy* or a *metaphor.*

- Use an *example* or an *anecdote.*

- The three Cs:

  - » Colorful words

  - » Clichés (Catchy phrases)

  - » Contemporary references

- Think *"quotable quotes."*

- *Take time* to think before responding (unless it's a "live" interview, pausing is perfectly acceptable).

- Begin with a *complete sentence* that can stand by itself.
- *Avoid jargon*—especially industry related terminology.
- Use words that most people understand. Remember, you are trying to reach the widest possible audience so your language needs to reflect that and be easily understood.

The magic of threes

You may have heard the phrase, "Third time's a charm." It certainly is when it comes to developing speeches and sound bites. It gives a rhythmic quality to your speech, helps emphasize your points and increases the memorability of your ideas. One thing to consider when planning a three-pronged statement is to make sure all three parts are approximately the same length and have a similar structure.

Examples:

"Veni, vidi, vici." (I came, I saw, I conquered.)
–Julius Caesar

"Be clear, be brief, be seated."
–Franklin Delano Roosevelt, 32nd President

"Government of the people, by the people, for the people."   –
–Abraham Lincoln

"The Good, the Bad, and the Ugly" –movie title

"Stop, Drop, and Roll." –Fire safety PSA

And on a lighter note:

"Wine, women, and song." –Martin Luther

Pairing and comparing

To compare or contrast is another technique that adds pizazz: *"We think we act because of how we FEEL...but we also feel because of how we ACT."* –Gretchen Rubin

"Ask not what your country can do for you, ask what you can do for your country." –John Fitzgerald Kennedy

Here's a quote I created to use when I teach fitness classes: *"It only feels good doing NOTHING when you have done SOMETHING!"*

I came up with this slogan for a local real estate agent: *"[Person's Name]—turning reality into reality."*

The power of repetition

Repetition is an extremely useful tool to help get your point across and again, to create a rhythm that is pleasing to the ear. It also can be a very useful way of hammering home an idea. Numerous scientific studies have verified that repeating a word, phrase or sound is an incredibly effective way to convince your audience that what you are saying is truthful.

As stated earlier in this book, when creating a message, you want to do the following: *"Tell them what you are going to tell them, tell them, then tell them what you told them."* Obviously, that was a blatant use of repetition but also a catchy way to help you remember what you need to do: use repetition.

A masterful example incorporating *many* of the above mentioned speaking styles is the "I have a dream" speech by Dr. Martin Luther King Jr.

"I have a dream that one day in Alabama, with its vicious racists, with its governor having his lips dripping with the words of interposition and nullification—one day right there in Alabama little black boys and black girls will

49

be able to join hands with little white boys and white girls as sisters and brothers.

"I have a dream today.

"I have a dream that one day every valley shall be exalted and every hill and mountain shall be made low, the rough places will be made plain, and the crooked places will be made straight..."

Here are a few examples of sound bites:

"If all you have is a hammer, then everything you want to hit will look like nails." –Abraham Maslow

"The traffic was so busy that crossing the road was like taking your life into your feet." –Anonymous

"I got into this business because there was a check in the right hand and an offer in the left." –Anonymous

"I was caught between a rock and a work place."
–Anonymous

"Glaucoma is the sneak thief of vision."
–American Academy of Ophthalmology

"Imagine the place on the map as a fist with a thumb; the wrist was where the fighting took place..." –AP reporter

"If you're only looking through the rearview mirror and not looking through the windshield, you're not seeing the whole view." –Various authors/variations, including Byrd Baggett and Joel Osteen

"Tinkering under the hood of government." –Henry Ross Perot

"The regime must decide whether they're for the ballot or the bullet."
–Oft quoted, original source: Malcolm X

"A blunt pencil is better than a sharp mind."
–Chinese proverb

"I am a pit bull on the pant leg of opportunity."
–George W. Bush

Regarding Affirmative Action—a good example of using imagery:

"If you have two fingers bruised and bleeding, by giving them attention you benefit the whole hand."
–Interview on NPR

"Sex appeal is 50 percent what you've got and 50 percent what people think you've got." –Sophia Loren

"For most of history "anonymous" was a woman."
–Virginia Wolfe

And here's a few from Franklin P. Jones:
(one of my go-to authors for witty quotes)

"Honest criticism is hard to take, particularly from a relative, a friend, an acquaintance or a stranger."

"You can learn many things from children. How much patience you have, for instance."

"It's a strange world of language in which skating on thin ice can get you into hot water."

"The trouble with being punctual is that nobody's there to appreciate it."

What are your favorite quotes or sound bites?

CHAPTER 12
Warnings and Reminders

- Make sure you know whether the show is live or prerecorded, and nowadays with digital, assume the camera is always on.

- If the interview is being prerecorded, and you find that the first thought that came out of your mouth is not exactly to your liking you might have the option to stop and start over. This would not be something to do repeatedly, just every now and then when you are really finding yourself *stepping in it*!

- Act naturally—if you need to cough, turn away from the microphone to clear your throat.

- *Phone interviews:* Ask if the interview is being recorded. In some locales, you have to be informed of this by the interviewer. A reporter cannot legally record an interview with you without your permission.

- *Print media:* Be careful. They can interview you on the phone, but they don't need your consent to print what you say. Never request to see an article or story before it is printed or aired as a prerequisite for doing the interview. However, it is totally okay to offer yourself as a proofreader when the reporter has finished working on the article (and I would advise you to do so).

- Sometimes it's a good idea to wait before returning a phone call from a reporter until you've collected your thoughts. But don't wait too long, otherwise they'll be getting the story from somebody else. Also, if you call back in a timely manner, you'll have a fighting chance of having your point of view put forth, as opposed to that of your competition.

- Don't guess at answers when you don't know. There is nothing wrong with saying "I don't know." Better yet, say, "I don't know, but I'll find out and get back to you" (and do it!). You can also refer the reporter to someone who can answer the question appropriately. Another choice is, "I don't know much about that, but what I do know is…" and go on with your prepared message.

- Avoid industry jargon and clichés. (i.e., "that's a great question") Every question is a great question.

- Do not allow yourself to be pigeonholed into either/or, or yes/no answers. Maintain control of the interview.

- There is no such thing as "off the record." Don't say anything to a reporter that you don't want repeated in the print media, on social media, or on television. A media representative is a reporter first and a friend second.

- Never lie to a reporter, and don't say "no comment." You might choose to lead the reporter in a different direction, or simply state you don't know the answer to a particular question. You might also mention that you are not at liberty to answer the question, especially if there is ongoing or pending litigation. Again, I encourage you to use every question as an opportunity to state what it is that you do know (aka *your message.*)

- Don't answer a question with a question.

- Don't argue with a reporter or lose your cool.

- Don't offer a free lunch, trip, or drink to a reporter. Reporters want stories, not payoffs.

CHAPTER 13
After the Interview

Before airing:

- If the interview is prerecorded or will be edited for a future airing or publication, be available to answer any last-minute questions or proofread the article if asked. Make sure your name and your organization are spelled correctly!

- Write a letter of thanks for the opportunity to participate, whether you truly enjoyed the experience or not. And offer your availability for future interviews.

After airing:

- You may be perfectly happy with the news coverage. In that case, let them know that you appreciated their efforts. Send a short note commending them, and send a copy to their editor or boss. This will help reporters remember you the next time they need a source.

- If it has already gone to print or aired, and you are not happy with the news story, you must decide if any follow-up is necessary. Don't write or call when you're angry about a story. Cool off first. Then, write a calm, friendly letter or email and point out where pertinent information was missed, what it was, or how you'd be glad to supply more information. If all else fails, request a retraction and copy the reporter's editor or manager on the correspondence.

And remember...

Paying for play is advertising.
Praying for play is media relations.

PART 2

Giving a Talk or Workshop with a Live Audience

CHAPTER 14
A Toolbox of Interactive Techniques

This section is intended for those presenting to a live audience, where there is an opportunity to interact with audience members. This is usually the role of somebody who is already well-versed in public speaking, but not *necessarily*. For expediency however, it will be assumed that you know the basics such as speaking with resonance and authority, and you are using hand gestures to emphasize what you are saying.

What is often missed when giving an interactive talk is the connectedness that can make a huge difference between your audience sitting on the edge of their seats or considering taking a power nap. Many speakers forget to make these invaluable connections with their audience throughout their talk and can sometimes unintentionally leave people out when asking questions or attempting to engage their audience. Let's take a look at my set of 17 favorite tools and techniques that can help make it less challenging and more fun to deliver a lively talk while keeping your audience engaged and connected.

CHAPTER 15
Look Around

When you first enter the stage or have just been introduced, before you say *anything*, make sure to look around the room at every person in the audience. This may take just a couple of seconds, however it is a very important first step in *setting the stage* and shows you have the confidence to acknowledge *everyone* who is there. It also sets a tone that you are not flustered or rushed and that you are comfortable in your own skin. *Even if you don't feel that way,* this is a very important and immediate way to create that impression.

If you have been introduced or edified already, it won't be necessary to reiterate your credentials and/or expertise; however it is safe to say that repetition is very powerful when it comes to public speaking, and repeating just the main points of who you are and why you are there is extremely valuable—especially if the person who introduced you was less than compelling with their edification of your achievements and experience.

CHAPTER 16
How to Begin

After your welcoming look around the room you will want to engage your audience with some questions that immediately capture their attention—something relating to your talk or it may even be regarding the weather or a location-based question…something that is easily relatable for *everyone*.

For instance, I am president of a women's business networking group and when I lead our monthly dinner meeting, I always ask folks at the beginning, "Who is new to our meeting tonight?" If the whim takes me, I might also ask the opposite to that question—something like, "Who is *not so* new?" Depending on the wine intake during the informal networking portion, that question might get a giggle because of the implied age reference. After that I will usually ask the newbies how they heard about our group and get a lot of interaction right up front. This format immediately has people feeling involved and comfortable.

Starting out the gate by asking a question or two is a great way to break the ice. After that, you can come back and re-state your name, welcome everyone, and repeat the title of your talk.

Next, look around the room once more and take the opportunity to again acknowledge everyone and express appreciation. For example, you could say that you realize there are many other places they could be (unless you are speaking at a prison) and thank them for taking the time out of their busy schedules to be here.

CHAPTER 17
Acknowledge Others

If you are giving a talk where you are one of several speakers, take the opportunity to edify and acknowledge the person who had just introduced you as well as your speaker colleagues. In preparation for this acknowledgment, make sure you are clear on how to say that person's name, checking the correct pronunciation, as well as double checking with them about their background and area of expertise.

An amusing aside, I once volunteered to be the announcer at a swim meet for my daughter's swim team. It was part of our parent responsibility to volunteer doing something for the team. I figured being the announcer would be a piece of cake, since I already know a couple of things about public speaking. The job was to announce over the microphone the name of every swimmer before each race. Easy, right? I could not have been more sorely mistaken. I did not know most of the kids, and virtually all of them had extremely difficult surnames to pronounce. I'm pretty sure I managed to offend almost everyone that day. It is something I will never forget—or do again. So, with that said, I strongly encourage you to check with the other speakers on name pronunciation.

CHAPTER 18
Consider All Sides

When you are asking a question of your audience, you always want to consider that there will be some people who raise their hands in response to the question you are asking, and others who may not. If you do not address both sides of that question you may leave the more reticent folks in the audience feeling that their experience is not valued or included in your talk…and therefore they may begin to tune out or ignore what you are saying.

For example, you might ask folks:

"Who got caught in that horrible traffic this morning?"

"Who didn't have any issues with the traffic?"

For this example, based on responses you might go on to interact with the lucky few who didn't get caught in the traffic jam by asking if they are staying in the hotel next door—or the optional, albeit slightly amusing, third part of this kind of questioning would be to say something like, *"And who won't answer my questions, no matter what I ask?"* whilst raising your hand yet again. It's corny, but always gets a bit of a chuckle. The main point is to get people interacting with you right away so they are more likely to sit forward and listen to what you have come to say.

CHAPTER 19
Hand Raising
and How to Deal with Questions

While we are on the hand raising conversation, I want to address a concern I often see. Since most speakers are a bit shy, when they do ask a question and correctly raise their hand up to signal participation, often, out of nervousness, they will rapidly bring their hand down without waiting for audience members to raise their hands and respond. This is a fine point but a very important distinction because you need to command the stage. You need to be at ease while holding your hand up. You need to look around and *wait*. Wait for people to raise their hands. It sends a message to the audience that it's okay for them to participate—and that participation is in fact expected.

Here's another scenario to discuss when dealing with the Q and A. Let's say you are asking a specific question or are inviting audience questions. Suppose several people have raised their hands to be chosen. You pick someone who catches your eye. Now what do you do? The natural instinct is to go closer to that person and engage with them, however, by doing so you are excluding the entire audience except for the folks sitting in the immediate area of the person asking the question. Instead, hear the comment or response, walk to the *opposite* side of the stage, and then acknowledge the questioner, repeat what they said, and respond with your comments. This way, you have not left everyone else in the audience out when you are having that communication between the person asking or answering a question. Everyone feels included.

If you have been asked a question and you may not know the answer *or* you would like to include even more audience participation, you might invite the audience to answer the question. Again, the more interaction, the more your presentation will come alive.

Furthermore, if someone has asked a question, and you (or someone else) has supplied an answer, then another courtesy would be to ask them if their question was answered. If they say *"no,"* this allows for clarification. If they say *"yes,"* thank them for the question and give them a hand. This gives closure and acknowledgement to the person who bravely interacted with you.

CHAPTER 20
Partner or Group Shares

One of the best-kept secrets in public speaking is that the less that you do, the more successful your presentation can often be. Most people in your audience are listening to the radio station WIIFM, which stands for "What's in it for me?" This comes back to *knowing your audience*. What this also means is that the more that members of your audience are involved and engaged with the topic you are discussing, the more they will feel that your talk was amazing and that they actually had a part in making it amazing. It's a win-win!

If you share an idea or concept, the standard lecture style would be to present in a scholarly manner, all of your points from beginning to end with no interaction. This is the typical professorial approach to public speaking (no offense to professors.) It often allows the audience to get a quick cat nap and is not necessarily effective communication. However, if you suggest a concept or questions for the audience, instead of having it all be about you and what you have to say, you could instead suggest that they turn to someone near them, each pair choose an A and a B, then have the A's raise their hands, also the B's (so you know everyone is on the same page,) and don't forget to ask if anyone doesn't have a partner and get them sorted.

Next, give them their marching orders—it may be something random to warm up the crowd like *"Ask your partner where they would like to go on vacation and why,"* or something relating specifically to your workshop or training. Create parameters so each person gets a set amount of time to do the task. Remind folks to "switch" and then you will also need to give them notice to wrap it up. Instead of using A and B, you could also use physical attributes such as hair length instead: "The person with the longest hair goes first," for example.

A further aspect to the partner or group share is then having one or two folks share what they learned, or what was the "take away" from the exercise they just did. Again, you will want to make sure that you raise your hand as a signal for people to also raise their hands and at the end always acknowledge that individual for sharing. Tell the audience to give them a round of applause, and begin clapping as a signal to do so. After that you could also ask the audience, "Who else can relate to what [insert volunteer's name] just said?" This also gives validation to the person who bravely spoke up and invites further discussion.

CHAPTER 21
Practice

I have worked with so many speakers who feel that they have their talk nailed down because they have read it over multiple times. However, *reading* to yourself and *speaking* out loud are two entirely different experiences. When you just read over your talk and feel like you know it inside-out, you are missing the point. The fact is, you need to stand up with good posture (or if sitting is your format, sit up straight) and practice *aloud*.

What I am talking about here is creating muscle memory versus just thinking it over in your head. When you say things out loud your brain remembers it in a different way—in the very same way that you will eventually be performing. With the capability that cell phone cameras now afford us, it is easy for you to practice and do a run-through with your phone or using an audio recording app, and then play it back. Practicing aloud and observing how your talk comes across is an essential part of good preparation.

Practice with friends, family members, or anyone who will give you the time of day. When you do practice with a captive audience, make sure they understand to hold feedback until you are ready to receive it. The reason is sometimes just getting your talk *on its feet* and stumbling through from beginning to end is the best way to build confidence and know that you can get all the way through it when push comes to shove—even if getting through it means faltering or needing to look down and review your notes.

CHAPTER 22
Take Breaks

Just because you are energized about your talk and can go for a long stretch without a break doesn't mean everyone else in your audience will be willing to. If your talk is more like a workshop or on the longer side of a lecture, you will need to factor in breaks for various reasons, such as hunger, stretching, bathroom breaks, checking messages, etc. If you don't factor in these breaks and embed them into your talk, people may become distracted or end up leaving and thus interrupt other audience members whilst doing so. Also, short breaks allow for audience networking and for folks to fully digest the meat of your topic—particularly if your talk contains dense information or requires a lot of mental focus.

During these short breaks, if there is a possibility to have music, play something upbeat and fun. When the music finishes it also can be a signal to those outside the room that it's time to come back and tune in again.

Another essential break is the stretch break. As we all know, it is not healthy for the body, or the brain, to stay in a seated position for an extended period. Why not combine "stretch breaks" with a small activity such as an assignment where audience members introduce themselves to a sphere of people around them or share why they came or where they are from. All of these techniques help get people out of their seat, out of their comfort zone and interacting with each other. The end result is that when they do sit back down, they will be more energized and engaged (and perhaps will have also made a new friend).

CHAPTER 23
Check In

Even when you are not necessarily asking a question that requires an answer, it is very important to make sure that the audience is *with you* and they really are following what you are saying. Using phrases such as *"Does this make sense?"* or *"Are you with me?"* or *"Do you follow?"* are all good ways of keeping people nodding and engaged. Checking in and creating this back-and-forth bond with your audience creates a two-way street. It assures you they are following along with what you are saying. As a bonus, it also lets you know that folks are still awake!

Although it doesn't necessarily pertain to giving a speech, my research into speech and audience retention uncovered a very interesting phenomenon with regard to the speed, content, and speech patterns of men versus women—and some surprising differences regarding gender.

One study found that men tend to put more information into a shorter period of time than women do. However, what is most noteworthy is why. It turns out that more often than not, even though many women are not as content driven as men (please note that these are generalizations based on the findings of the study), what women do spend their time on during a conversation is checking in with the other person (their audience) to verify that they are understood.

So perhaps the truism "quality, not quantity" is especially accurate with female speakers. After all, what good is it to get more information out, if your audience retains less of it? Those who might fit into the category of *verbose* (be it male or female) please take heed— ask yourself, *"Am I mostly focused on getting a lot of facts and talk-time in?"* or *"Am I checking to see if what I am saying is being received and understood by my audience?"*

CHAPTER 24
Using the Senses

Using as many of your senses as possible is a very effective way to make a powerful impact on your audience. This includes visuals such as props, imagery, handouts, using energetic music during breaks, and at even the simplest level, adjusting the lighting in the room. If people are breaking into groups or doing a brief partner share, you may want to have the lights come up a little in the auditorium so they can see each other more easily; then have the lights go down when it is time to wrap up and return their attention to you.

CHAPTER 25
It Takes a Village

Did you ever have a teacher who was really intelligent, but who was horrible at sharing what he or she knew? I did. Knowing *a lot* of *things* doesn't always equate to being a brilliant speaker. Sometimes those with the *most* knowledge are not necessarily the best communicators. Take comfort in finding ways to get across what you *do know*, what you have to share, and make it come alive for your audience by allowing collective participation.

By understanding that you will never know all the answers, and that nobody does, should provide some relief. Sadly, many shy away from speaking for fear that they don't know *everything* or they don't know *enough*. Granted, you will probably know more about your topic than most people in your audience, but there will always be something that you may not know or remember. If this is the case, it's a good idea to include the audience—let it become a team effort.

I recently gave a talk about public speaking in the film industry called, "How to be *seen* when you work behind the *scenes*." During the Q and A, a question came to me that I couldn't exactly relate to. The person asking the question had obviously experienced something that I had not. It was along the lines of whether I had noticed that male producers treat me differently compared to female producers when I was being interviewed to work on film projects. My honest frame of reference was that I had not noticed this in an across-the-board pattern, so I responded that in each instance I was treated differently based on the individual interviewing me, not on their gender.

However, I did not want to diminish the questioner's experience, so I asked what they had encountered. Sure enough, the responder had a very specific example in mind and shared that. It was valuable because that person got acknowledgement for their exact experience, what they were referring to, and at the same time it furthered the collective conversation. It also enhanced the conversation and gave voice to others in the audience who may have had similar encounters.

CHAPTER 26
Don't Assume

Hopefully, you will have an eager audience, listening with bated breath to your every utterance. Even though you are the expert, which is why you are on stage—and even though you have the credibility and audience attention—it is easy to fall into the assumption that *everybody* wants your coaching. However, that is *not* always the case. It is never wise to assume that what you have to share is wanted by all. If it ever comes down to an instance where somebody is asking a question where your response might move into the realm of being personal for the questioner, it's always good form to first to ask permission before offering coaching or making a personal suggestion. For example, you might ask, *"Would you be open to some feedback?"* or *"Would you like a suggestion?"*

I teach a yoga-pilates class part-time and even though there are many instances where folks need my help with correcting their form, I *always* ask their permission first by saying something like, *"Are you okay if I touch you/help you straighten your spine?"* From time to time I have had some individuals decline assistance. We don't know what is going on with people so *never* assume…or as the insightful Pooh Bear once said, *"You never can tell with bees!"*

CHAPTER 27
Voice and Pacing

One way to captivate your audience is with your use of voice. By changing the pacing and the volume of your voice and by thinking about where you want to put the emphasis, you will keep folks not only awake but also engaged. I always remind my clients "underline your words with your voice." Choose the places in your talk that you want to stand out by placing emphasis on those words or concepts—this will help bring your ideas to life.

Another technique for creating impact is using pauses right after you make an important statement. Pausing adds power—it will help what you just said sink in. Also when you pause, use that opportunity to look around and connect with your audience. By pausing and looking around you are really asking your audience, *"Do you get how powerful this is?"* It will seal the deal and maximize the impact of what you just said.

The speed of your speech is another aspect of your talk that can make it dramatically more memorable to your audience. There are mixed studies on this, but most of them point to the following: If a person is speaking in a slow, paced, almost methodical manner, then they are perceived to be more intelligent than those who speak rapidly. One reason is, when you speak more slowly it conveys that you have more confidence (even if you don't). Using an intentionally slower pace of speaking also counters the fact that most people speed up when they talk in front of an audience—particularly when they are nervous. Intentionally slowing down, pacing yourself, is a wise choice to balance out that tendency. People will think you are smarter (even if you are not,) you will come across as being more confident, and the listener will be better able to take in and process what you are saying.

The *only* time that this is not an effective technique is when you are speaking to an adverse audience—an audience that is not a fan of yours or of what you have to say. In this instance, it works in your favor to speak quickly because the audience is so focused on trying to keep up with what you are saying that they have less time to formulate counterarguments.

Depth of voice is another consideration to add to the toolkit of techniques. Did you realize that people who have a deeper voice are perceived to be more authoritative, competent, and trustworthy? At first glance this may sound like a sexist bias based on men's voices usually being deeper than women's, and men often being in a position of authority and power (which has been the status quo for no less than 6,000 years). However, it has also been shown to be true in the animal kingdom, among primates, frogs, and some birds. When wanting to assert dominance or authority, a deeper voice is often called upon. So perhaps this phenomenon—this preference for respecting deeper resonant voices—is born from a primal source encoded in our being.

Regardless of the reason, speaking in a lower tone projects confidence and authority, so this is certainly something to con-sider if your voice has a higher pitch and you want to be taken more seriously. Granted, there is only so much that can be done, based on physiology, to add depth to a voice, but with breathing and voice exercises, it can be achieved. For example, Margaret Thatcher underwent this sort of intense speech training at the Royal National Theatre before her election in 1979. This helped lower her pitch and develop a calm, authoritative tone which many say helped to advance her political career.

Does a higher pitched voice put women at a disadvantage? That depends. Consider these interesting findings from a study by Cecilia Pemberton at the University of South Australia. Turns out women's voices have dropped by 23 hertz since women have been more widely employed in the workforce. The researchers analyzed the voices of two groups of Australian women aged 18 to 25 years. They compared archived recordings of Australian women talking back in 1945, contrasting with the recordings of women taken in the early 1990s. Even factoring in considerations such as the pill and smoking, the researchers still found the frequency had substantially dropped from an A-sharp below middle C, to approximately G-sharp.

What does this all mean? Since women have been making their way in the workforce, perhaps women have unconsciously been lowering their voice in order to be taken more seriously. I don't claim that this is the case, but based on these findings, it is certainly worth musing upon.

If you would like to work on lowering your voice, then one route is to seek the assistance of a good voice coach. There are also many reputable theater training programs offering voice classes that incorporate breathing exercises and techniques that help you find your breath so your voice projects from your abdomen as opposed to your throat or head. These techniques do help to deepen your voice and maintain a calmer demeanor.

CHAPTER 28
Tell Stories

"Facts tell, stories sell" says it all. As a people, we have been encultur-ated through thousands of years with storytelling as our main source of learning. It is embedded in us. It is one of the most effective tools of public speaking. Just make sure your story has what we in media like to call "take-home pay." Make sure your story has some kind of "a-ha! moment" at the end to wrap up. Provide an example of what you have been discussing. Use it as a way to deepen, embellish or bring to life a concept, or as a way to use repetition in your talk without saying the same thing over and over again.

For example, if you were a dentist giving a talk about dental hygiene to a business networking group, and you were making a case for how important it is to get a checkup every six months, you could share a story of a patient who decided to skip their regular checkup and what happened to them. *"Erosion or corrosion of the teeth can be a sign of leukemia,"* for instance. Or perhaps someone who came in for a checkup, not realizing there was anything wrong, found out they not only had gum disease but that this was an early warning sign that they also were pre-diabetic. And if they had not come in, it may have taken years to detect and by then, major damage would have been done. I always advocate for putting a positive spin on the outcome (if possible) but fear and stories of what went wrong can also be powerful motivators. Segue your story into why, in this instance, *"getting regular dental checkups"* is so important.

CHAPTER 29
Overcoming Fear

Have you ever experienced a *"Beam me up, Scotty"* moment when you were the speaker? (For those too young to remember, that was a *Star Trek* reference.) You get out in front of an audience (or camera) and suddenly you have the urge to be transported off of this planet and be somewhere, anywhere, far, far away. If you are nodding emphatically, you are in good company. Most people undergo this "out of body" experience, especially when they are relatively new to giving a speech. Much of this is triggered by concern over how you are coming across, whether you are doing it *right* and whether your listeners will find you likable. Those thoughts playing in the back of your mind compete for "brain time," detracting from what you had prepared to say in your talk. If you allow them to dominate, they can literally take you out of the game.

So, what can you do? This is the top question clients ask me, how to handle those nerves and self-doubt. One of the most effective remedies I have found to help overcome all of these thoughts and fears is simply becoming aware of *where* you are putting your focus. When our focus is on ourselves, when we are judging our own performance, it inhibits our ability to truly be in the moment. Ultimately it can cause us to forget what we came to say and reinforce the dreaded message we say to ourselves, *"I suck at this!"* or *"Everyone hates me!"*

This may sound simple but it is practically magic. When you put your focus on your audience, on helping others, and really being of service, it will change *everything.*

Say to yourself mantras such as:
"I am here to help."
"I am here to give these folks great information."
"I am excited to be here."
"I am delighted to be given this opportunity to share what I know."

CHAPTER 30
The Elephant in the Room

Inevitably during your *"career"* as a speaker you will find situations that cannot be ignored. A novice at public speaking might *try* to pretend that the awkward or unexpected moment, the "elephant in the room," is not happening or did not happen; however a skilled speaker will acknowledge what is happening and hopefully think on their feet and turn it into a point of humor or an opportunity to create a deeper rapport with their audience. Sometimes these "being in the moment" scenarios allow a *real* opportunity for connection between the speaker and the audience that would not have happened if the speaker was to continue to plow on and stay "on script."

I once gave a talk that was held in a private room in the back of a pub. Obviously it was not a professional environment—there was no stage and I was halfway parked between a wall and a window, with tables and chairs all around. At one point an audience member interrupted me and asked me to move over by the wall so I could be seen better without the window as a backdrop. This observation of course was only relative to where that particular audience member was sitting, not necessarily the experience of everyone in the room.

On the first interruption, I welcomed the suggestion and tried to accommodate, however I was squeezed into a spot beside a chair that was slightly in my way, and during some of the animated moments in my talk, I would inch back in front of the window. On the second interruption I thanked the person again and then added that sometimes being a silhouette wasn't such a bad thing, especially once you get to be of a certain age. The audience found my response amusing and I did not hear another interruption from that audience member for the rest of the event.

I use humor to quell what might otherwise become a disruptive situation. And oftentimes earn a good laugh in the process. *"When life gives you lemons, make lemonade."* This old adage is valuable to consider when the unexpected arises. Use what is going on with your audience, use what is happening in the here and now, and make that a part of either what you're talking about or perhaps use it to make light of a situation so that it doesn't drag down the energy in the room.

Use it, especially when the person creating an elephant-in-the-room is you! Perhaps you forgot what you were going to say or you dropped something. Best thing to do is acknowledge what just happened. You could say, *"I'm a bit of a klutz when I'm nervous,"* or *"I completely forgot what I was going to say! Don't you hate that?"* and share your humanity with those in attendance.

By getting real, your audience will want to be on your side and root for you. More often than not, they want you to succeed and certainly will be more encouraged when you are honest with them about what is going on. In some instances, you might even ask the audience for help.

Questions like:

"Now what was I just saying?"

"Do you mind passing me the clicker?"

"Who here has had that happen to them?"

I witnessed this at a talk I attended recently. The speaker was distracted by something and then when trying to get back on track, got lost. Without skipping a beat, they said, *"I completely forgot what I was talking about."* They were immediately prompted by several eager members of the audience and effortlessly jumped back into the talk. The whole incident occurred seamlessly, adding a humility that was endearing.

CHAPTER 31
Have Fun

Finally, regardless of what your talk is about, find joy in what you're doing, or at least project the impression that you want to be there, and want to share knowledge that stands to benefit your audience. Set this as your mantra: *"I am delighted to be here!"* That mindset will shine through!

All of these suggestions are simply tools in your toolbox. Sometimes you may need a drill and sometimes you may only need a pair of pliers…but at some point, you are going to need most of them. By being ready and knowing when and how to use these tools, you will become a speaker that not only is unafraid to give a talk, you will become a speaker who, dare I say, relishes speaking opportunities. My advice to you is get out there, share what you know with the world, help others, and have fun!

HOW TO HANDLE PEOPLE
Oratory and public speaking is an art which **must be learned.** Don't you believe bunk about ''natural born'' speakers! For your greater personal advancement let this excellent course teach you the fundamentals of influencing people: how to make them laugh, cry and ACT. Only **$3.95.** Circle **No. 3** in coupon below. Satisfaction or refund.

The Public Speaking image is the copyright property of Quantity Postcards, Oakland CA.

RESOURCES

Here is a partial list of business groups and associations for speaking opportunities.

TOASTMASTERS

Toastmasters International is a non-profit educational organization that teaches public speaking and leadership skills through a worldwide network of clubs. Visit their website for more information.

NATIONAL SPEAKERS ASSOCIATION

The National Speakers Association (NSA) is the premier organization for professional speakers.

There is a fee to join. However, if you are wanting to take your speaking career to the next level, this would be a valuable organization to participate in. The NSA empowers speakers to thrive and influence. They elevate excellence, share expertise, and challenge one another to constantly improve. To learn more or to join, visit their website at JoinNSA.com.

NSA is offering my readers a discount to join. Use promo code **OTR2019** to save $75 off your first year of membership. There is no expiration on this offer.

CHAMBER OF COMMERCE

In every city in the United States, as well as many other countries around the globe, there is a chamber of commerce (or equivalent).

They have several program meetings a month and frequently use speakers on a variety of topics.

According to the official World Chambers Network website, "The goal of any chamber is to help to further the interests of small businesses in a local area. The chamber of commerce gives you the opportunity to meet with other local business owners and network. Currently, there are about 13,000 chambers registered in the official World Chambers Network registry. There are roughly 4,000 chambers of commerce in the United States".

SERVICE CLUBS

Every week, service clubs like Kiwanis, Rotary, and Soroptimist International have regular meetings and these groups are always looking for speakers.

INDUSTRY SPECIFIC ASSOCIATIONS

Every industry has at least one association they are affiliated with. Here are some examples:

Women's Council of Realtors

National Association of Realtors

National Association of Black Accountants

Sales and Marketing Executives International

Financial Women's Association

Association for Financial Professionals

Most of these groups have monthly meetings, as well as annual, semi-annual, or quarterly conferences and conventions. There are *plenty* of speaking opportunities if you have knowledge to share that would be useful to that specific industry.

UNIVERSITY EXTENSIONS

Contact the various academic institutions in your area. Each of these offers classes to the public taught by professionals. Depending on your talents and skills, you could potentially be one of their instructors. This is a great way to establish professional credibility.

PROFESSIONAL ASSOCIATIONS

There are hundreds of thousands of groups around the globe that are not specific to a particular industry. These types of organizations are also looking for qualified speakers.

Here are just a few of a wealth of well-known groups:

Business Roundtable

BNI

Young Entrepreneur Council

Startup Grind

Vistage

HOLD YOUR OWN EVENT

Consider holding your own event to educate the public about your cause or organization. You could host an event in your office or in a rented room in a hotel for that matter. Regardless of your skill level, the best way to win as a speaker is to define your message, get coaching, and speak *on as many and varied occasions as you can*!

ABOUT THE AUTHOR

Andrea Devaux is a quintessential renaissance woman. Her eclectic career includes spending time as a public speaker and media coach; film maker; theatre director; fitness instructor; author; president and co-founder of a women's business networking group; and last but not least: mother.

In her formative years, she trained at the New Zealand Actors Theatre Studio, a Stanislavsky-based drama school. She then left her birthplace of New Zealand and cycled and sailed around the world—a trip that lasted almost five years, where she eventually found her heart and home in San Francisco, California. Her media career began when she was working for a major medical organization, training high-powered doctors to prepare for appearances on primetime television. Afterwards she transitioned into the position of on-staff media trainer for Media Alliance of San Francisco, while in the evenings she worked with local actors directing theatre and sketch comedy in downtown San Francisco.

It was during this time that Andrea astutely observed that her theatre productions only reached a small subset of the population, so she set her sights on film production, collaborating on projects with a much wider-reaching, global medium. For over two decades she has worked as a script continuity supervisor for commercials, feature films, and episodic television. More recently she has worked as a director for commercials and web-based media.

With her theatre training, directing skills, and media coaching background, Andrea brings a unique perspective on how to help her clients come alive, stand out from the crowd, and enjoy the experience of public speaking. She currently works with individuals and groups who need to finesse how to stay on message, or for that matter, figure out what their message is.

ACKNOWLEDGMENTS

Special thanks to Kitty Baker, who helped comb out a few kinks from my grammar and my Kiwi vernacular to make this book more readable. I so appreciate her support.

I wish to also acknowledge my partner, Leslie Cornelius, who has been a huge support to me—not to mention having endured, listened to, and read through multiple versions of this book. Thank you, honey.